POETIC VOYAGES CHEADLE

Edited by Allison Dowse

First published in Great Britain in 2001 by
YOUNG WRITERS
Remus House,
Coltsfoot Drive,
Peterborough, PE2 9JX
Telephone (01733) 890066

HB ISBN 0 75433 164 4
SB ISBN 0 75433 165 2

FOREWORD

Young Writers was established in 1991 with the aim to promote creative writing in children, to make reading and writing poetry fun.

This year once again, proved to be a tremendous success with over 88,000 entries received nationwide.

The Poetic Voyages competition has shown us the high standard of work and effort that children are capable of today. It is a reflection of the teaching skills in schools, the enthusiasm and creativity they have injected into their pupils shines clearly within this anthology.

The task of selecting poems was therefore a difficult one but nevertheless, an enjoyable experience. We hope you are as pleased with the final selection in *Poetic Voyages Cheadle* as we are.

CONTENTS

Hursthead Junior School

Michael Edge	68
Megan Biggar	69
Lauren Gill	70
Jennifer King	71
James Cresswell	72
James Thornley	73
Verity Rushton	74
Robert Blease	75
Jack Moores	76
Rebecca Thomas	77
Tristan Russell	78
Charles Hartle	79
Bethany Williams	80
Adam Crowder	81
Olivia McGahey	82
Charlie Amos-Brown	83
Stephanie Lee	84
Becky Dawson	85
Sophie Fletcher	86
Chris Russell	87
Oliver Bristow	88
Nicola Macleod	89
Elizabeth Bateman	90
Adam Ramsden-Smith	91
Anna Louise Peate	92
Hayley Ramsden	93
Sam Roe	94
Kate Earnshaw	95
Benjamin Devereux	96
Sophie Dyde	97
Jack Green	98
Matthew Oates	99
Philip Moorhouse	100
Matthew Drury	101
Emma Taylor	102

The Poems

DREAMER

I'm a superstar,
I've got a flashy car.
Hollywood, I'm there,
It's like walking on air.
I'm on TV
And in all the Soaps,
Holding high my big, big hopes.
I've got a fancy dress,
Who cares about the mess?
I'm going out
Without a doubt,
Out with the King
And the Queen.
Oh look there's
My bed,
It was all just a dream!

Emma Addison (10)
Brookhead Junior School

UNTITLED

Red is the colour of a poppy swaying in the sun.
Blue is the colour of the sea shimmering with glee.
White is the colour of the clouds fluttering in the sky.
Yellow is the colour of the light shimmering nice and bright.
Green is the colour of a meadow just like a picturesque scene.

Danielle Houghton (10)
Brookhead Junior School

THE KOALA

A button nose,
And funny shaped toes.
A home in the trees
With the eucalyptus leaves.
I look like a bear
But I'm very rare.
I don't make a sound
And I don't run around.
I live a long way away
Where my night is your day.

Lauren Sharp (9)
Brookhead Junior School

BLUE

The sea shivers me
in a wavy way,
it ebbs and flows,
it crashes and bashes
on its beachy bay.
A slush is ice bits,
it makes my tongue
go very numb,
my favourite flavour
in the world is
bubblegum.

Katie Goodacre (10)
Brookhead Junior School

THE SOUND COLLECTOR (AT SCHOOL)
(Based on The Sound Collector by Roger McGough)

A stranger called this morning
Dressed all in black and grey,
Put every sound into a bag
And carried them away.

The clicking of the PC,
The clanging of the chair,
The scraping of the pencil,
The sweeping of Mrs Hare.

The closing of a book,
The bouncing of a ball,
The ringing of a phone,
The angel singing in the hall.

The collecting of the food,
The jingling of the fork,
The chattering of the children,
The chewing of the pork.

The swooshing of the flying birds,
The zooming of the cars,
The children playing with their friends
Saying thanks and ta's.

A stranger called this morning
He didn't leave his name,
Left us only silence,
Life will never be the same.

Jake Jones (10)
Brookhead Junior School

THE DOG

A good - jumper
A brilliant - bumper
A cat - scarer
A toy - tearer
A noisy - barker
A nosy - parker
A heavy -sleeper
A bird - eater
A mailman - chaser
A good - racer
A great - fighter
A bum - biter.

Matthew Maddison (10)
Brookhead Junior School

THE SOUND COLLECTOR
(Based on The Sound Collector by Roger McGough)

A stranger called this morning
Dressed all in black and grey,
Put every sound into a bag
And carried them away.

The bubbling of water,
The creaking of the lock,
Squeaking of the kettle,
The ticking of a clock.

The spreading of the water,
The ticking of the grill,
Munching of the toast
As the crumbs start to fall.

When you do the washing-up,
The swishing of the plates,
The splashing noise it makes,
The gurgle of the drain.

A stranger called this morning
He didn't leave his name,
Left us only in silence,
Life will never be the same.

Olivia McGough (10)
Brookhead Junior School

THE SOUND COLLECTOR
(Based on The Sound Collector by Roger McGough)

A stranger called this morning
Dressed all in black and grey,
Put every sound into a bag
And carried them away.

The bubbling of a fish,
The howling of a dog,
The scratching of a hamster,
The croaking of a frog.

The banging of some music,
The shutting of a door,
The noises of a TV,
The scrubbing of the floor.

The pinging of the microwave,
Mum making my tea,
The brewing of the kettle
And a cup of tea for me.

The patter of the raindrops,
The toast under the grill,
The running of the bathtub
As it starts to fill.

The bees work hard
To make their honey,
And we work hard
To make our money.

A stranger called in this morning,
He didn't leave his name,
Left us only silence,
Life will never be the same.

Katie Tatlock (10)
Brookhead Junior School

THE SEA

Waves come dashing, crashing, fast and slow,
Sometimes high and sometimes low
On their journey to the beach,
Will they get where they want to reach?

Swimming through the deep blue sea
You will see creatures if you come with me,
Shimmery goldfish and the creepy crab,
The way seals move is simply fab.

In the dark evil bottom of the sea
You will see sharks if you come with me.
The great white shark with big sharp teeth
Playing with his boat in the sea, oh no
Watch out Keith.

Jessica Davis (9)
Brookhead Junior School

Untitled

One wrinkly wombat wrestled white wellies while winking wisely
at a wasp.
Two timid toucans tirelessly tease terrifying tigers.
Three threatening thesauruses thump thoughtfully through the forest.
Four ferocious felines fight fearlessly for freedom.
Five fancy fish flap through flooded fish bowls.
Six sizzling sausages slap spotted sloths skilfully.
Seven sparkling salamanders slurp scrumptious champagne smoothly.
Eight enormous elephants eat enjoyable eggs elegantly.
Nine naughty newts nibble numb noses noisily.
Ten tropical tortoise tiptoe through tainted tunnels tiredly.

Felicity Parsons (10)
Brookhead Junior School

THE DINNER DISH REPORT

There he is walking to the table,
Shaking,
The fork in one hand,
Knife in the other,
Sweat coming down his cheek,
The contestant is sitting down,
The referee blows it!
He starts with the peas,
Flicks it up in the air,
And lands in his mouth, superb skill,
He moves onto the burger,
Oh yes.
He chews it up like it just isn't there!
Now he slices the potato in half,
Oh and here comes the gravy,
And he quickly changes tactics and picks up a spoon,
He slurps it up,
Perfect,
They think it's all over, it is now,
With a great time of 0.11 seconds.
Well I guess that's it from me,
Des Lynam,
And I'll see you on the next commentary on
The Dinner Dish Report,
Good night.

Jason Jones (9)
Brookhead Junior School

SOUNDS

The ringing of the doorbell,
The miaowing of the cat,
The rustling of the letters,
As they fall upon the mat.

The swishing of the curtain,
The shutting of the door,
The music from the stereo,
Vibrates across the floor.

The rattle of the milk bottles
Put out for the night
Pullling down the night shades
Darkness, switching off the light.

Mary Hirst (9)
Brookhead Junior School

A BULL-MASTIFF DOG

A mouth of blades,
A coat of different shades,
A swishing tail,
A paw with a missing nail,
A rugby ball shaped head,
A rough smelly bed,
A fast running beast,
A coat full of fleas,
A vicious growl,
A hobby chasing owls,
A bull-mastiff dog.

Carl Eden (10)
Brookhead Junior School

DOG

A good runner
A gentle lover
A lead breaker
A chocolate taker

A moon howler
A proud prowler
A lazy sleeper
A sly peeper
A cool pouncer
A high bouncer

A door yapper
An afternoon napper
A wet nose
Clipped toes

A quick walker
A rabbit stalker
Ears listening
Eyes glistening

A fast swimmer
A nail glimmer.

Hannah Cooper (9)
Brookhead Junior School

CAT

A mouse catcher
A wall scratcher
A proud walker
A bad talker
A lazy sleeper
A sly peeper
A cunning leaper
A funny eater
A rare weeper
A furry creature
A nine life cheater.

Jonathon Haley (9)
Brookhead Junior School

THE BULLY

She was standing very tall with
Her shoulders firmly back,
Eyes thin like thunder, one arm on her hip.
No one dared to move a lip
While they passed her ground.

She was standing with the rest,
Thinking she's the best,
When really she's a pest,
She should be forgotten.

She was standing in the middle,
Making such a fuss.
You don't want to know what about,
Make-up, hair styles, that kind of stuff.

She was looking all around
For someone to pick on.
I hope she doesn't see me,
Phew, she hasn't.

Ruth Emery (9)
Brookhead Junior School

MUSHROOMVILLE

Mushroomville is a really great place,
It's located in a really great space.
The village is around a tree,
It really is a sight to see.

Under the ground and down beneath,
There's a little guy called Little Leaf.
He decided he didn't like the mud,
He told his friends, they understood.

After he'd travelled all day and night,
The warm, bright sun came into sight.
He saw a light above the mud,
He knew he'd get there, he knew he would!

Leaf crawled and crawled for a few hours more,
He was up on the ground and there he saw,
A big sign saying 'Mushroomville',
'All I have to do is climb this hill.'

He climbed till he was up to the top,
Then he had a little stop.
Just to his horror and his fright,
Another great hill was in his sight.

Then just when he could take no more,
A mole stuck his head out from a camouflaged door.
He said 'How are you doing mate?
You look like you're in a terrible state.'

'Yes I want to climb this hill,
To the lovely Mushroomville.'
He flung Leaf onto his back,
Like a mini Santa's sack.

They bounced and leapt mile after mile
And to their horror they came to a style.
They dug and dug then they came up,
Underneath a buttercup.

'This is it you can leave me now,
I'll stay in Mushroomville from now.'
That's the end or so to say,
Leaf stayed in Mushroomville from that very day.

Emily Aris (9)
Bruntwood Primary School

THE YEAR OF SEASONS

Winter's cold and frosty,
the icicles on my toes.
It's spring and summer's coming,
that's when Nana sews.
In summer it's all hot
and sweat trickles down my nose.
In autumn leaves fall off
and Dad goes for a doze.
That's the year gone by,
it's time to start again,
so go away and enjoy
all the seasons once again.

Thomas Pryce (9)
Bruntwood Primary School

WOODLAND LIFE

In autumn, my favourite treat
Is walking in the woods,
With leaves under my feet
And a fox running by, as it should.
Badgers I can hear
But I rarely see,
The bushes rustle quite near,
I wonder what it can be?
Creeping, crawling on the ground,
Animals roaming free,
Look at all the bugs I've found,
In the trunk of this old tree.
Hundreds of ants are busy all day
Scurrying here and there,
Spiders waiting for their prey
To come into their lair.
When I look up to the sky
Birds fly from tree to tree,
I wish I was up so high,
Fly away to be free.
I really love this time of year
When summer is at an end,
I love to wander in the woods,
With all my woodland friends.

Rebecca Howard (10)
Bruntwood Primary School

MAGICAL POEM

I went into a shop,
To buy a little top,
But something strange happened
When I got to the door.
There was something that I saw,
There behind the desk was a little goblin,
He was all green,
But he didn't look mean.
I walked right up to him and touched him,
To my surprise he took my hand
And led me to a magical land.
We found ourselves
In a goblins' magical land,
They were rushing about this tiny place,
Making potions, stirring pots,
Knock knock that's what they say lots.
Go out another door,
To the outside world,
The shining sun or the balls they hurled,
Playing on the bright green grass,
Candy on trees and lots of nice flowers,
Little men climbing towers.
I let go of the goblin's hand,
I went off roaming . . .
Down the hill through the passage,
Rides and shops I had found . . .
Down the alley underground.
I walked into a shop
And I found:
The top I wanted to mind.
Out the shop I went,
Out to the magical land.

I needed to go,
So I said goodbye and . . .
Bang, bang, bang!
I'm back in the shop
With the little green man.

Rosie Teer (9)
Bruntwood Primary School

MY TEACHER!

My teacher is a creature with an unusual feature,
She's got long nails and broke the scales.
With a big fat nose and twenty-four toes,
She has hairy legs and eats rotten eggs.
When she stares us kids get scared,
When she's in a mood, when she speaks she's rude.
She has a tall hat and big black cat,
Someone whispered, 'She's a witch with a twitch
And very, very rich.'

She did a quick spell, but then I heard the bell,
I ran right past my teacher in the hope I could beat her,
To the playground where a kid,
Was so scared that he had hid,
In a dirty, grotty bin with a lid made of tin.

She had screamed at him for talking,
Running instead of walking,
Sitting at the back and hitting his friend Jack.
He'd done lots of naughty things -
Giggling during hymns, pouring water on the floor,
Painting on a door, eating food in class,
Skidding on the grass.

He really is a pain I just cannot explain
How awful he can be,
To all my friends and me.
I'd come outside to warn him
That our teacher was going to scorn him,
But while I was searching,
For the naughty little urchin,
I thought how he'd behaved,
He didn't deserve to be saved

And though our teacher's *mad,*
She isn't all that bad.
So I left him in the bin,
Even though it was a sin!

Lauren Clark (9)
Bruntwood Primary School

A MAGICAL ADVENTURE IN A MAGICAL LAND

A n adventure that I'm about to tell,

M agical like this adventure,
A ll aboard as we travel on our way,
G iants that we might meet on our trip,
I nside the magical land,
C andy that grows on the trees,
A nimals magical too,
L itres of fizzy pop falling from the sky like rain,

A pples all juicy and ripe,
D im lights all through the night,
V ery nice people that live in this land,
E normous elephants roaming far and wide,
N ight-time always busy and bright,
T offee apples growing from the ground,
U nicorns with bright shining horns,
R aspberry ripple ice cream houses,
E ggs with chocolate inside,

I ce castles all silvery and white,
N arnia, you can get there from here,

A ntelope graceful and proud.

M ysteries never to unfold,
A ardvarks with very long snouts,
G limmering pools full of water,
I mps tiny and good,
C ows that fly through the air with pink and purple spots,
A mber stones dotted here and there,
L akes some fathoms deep,

L and that is everywhere,
A labama fudge cake that grows in rows,
N ew flowers every day,
D onkeys blue and yellow in colour.

Now we must leave this magical land.
Dream and you are home and . . .
Boom!
We're home.

Sophie Simmons (9)
Bruntwood Primary School

SPRING

Spring is amazing,
The warm sun is blazing,
I see the birds in their nests,
Today they are taking a rest.

There are tall, tall trees
And the grass is up to my knees.
I see the daffodils swaying,
In the soft evening breeze.

Natalie Barnett (9)
Greenbank School

SPRING

Spring is bright and it is fun
To play out in the sun.
Spring wipes away the winter gloom
And flowers start to bloom.
It's like a witch with a wand
Who wipes the ice off the pond
No more frosty winds and no more icy blasts
The sun shows the promise of summer days to come.
I love to hear the birds in the morning,
Now as day is dawning.

Phoebe Bates (9)
Greenbank School

SPACE

The whooshing of comets,
Going through the dark sky.
The solar system is still,
All nine planets spinning
As they go round the sun.
Pluto is the smallest of them all
It is very hard to see.
Jupiter is the biggest
It is very clear to see.
The moon is the brightest
Of all nine planets.
If I was up there,
I would be able to see the earth
From thousands of miles away.
I wish I was up there,
But, maybe I will be someday.

Charlotte Bryan (10)
Greenbank School

NATURE

Nature is bright and green,
Nature is colourful and beautiful,
It brightens the world,
With its plants and trees
And buzzing bees,
It livens up our day,
In its wonderful way,
That's nature to me.

Danielle Cree (10)
Greenbank School

MY GARDEN

G is for garden, bright as can be,
A is for animals which follow me,
R is for the roses, which scent words can't describe,
D is for the den which the badgers enjoy life in,
E is for earwigs which crawl on brightly coloured flowers,
N is for nightingales singing in the trees.

Nicola Deakin (9)
Greenbank School

SPRING IS

S   pring is golden and lots of colours everywhere,
P   rimroses are blooming in the clear air.
R   oses are budding and growing,
I   rises of many colours, white, blue and yellow.
N   ectar is being sucked up by bees,
G   nats have all been waiting for spring to come.

I   s the summer coming soon?
S   pring is my favourite season.

Jane Donnan (9)
Greenbank School

SPRING

Spring is when baby lambs are born,
The daffodils are as bright as corn.
The grass is sprouting from the ground,
Everywhere I go I can hear a new sound.
The plants are growing
And the farmers are sowing.
There are leaves on the trees
And there's a nice warm breeze.
Spring is all around.

Kate Holroyd (9)
Greenbank School

SPRING

Spring is dawning
And the birds sing in the morning.
People are eating tasty corn,
While others are smelling the freshly cut lawn.

I am sitting in a little corner,
Wishing I was in a steaming hot sauna
But I am very happy here
Because summer is not far . . .
but near.

Felicity Khouri (9)
Greenbank School

THE MIGHTY BATTLE

Far off east, as far as you can go,
Through the mist and fog,
There is a smaller sun although hotter than ours,
A castle on a hill, a mighty roar, a forest on fire.
From the mist there roams a mighty horntail,
With spikes on his back and head,
A fire of blue around him,
Freezes me in fear.
A boy only with a wand opposes him bravely,
He mutters something,
A broom floats towards him,
He climbs on then kicks off the ground,
Rising, rising, rising higher than the dragon itself,
Then he yelled, 'Petrificustotalus'
And the dragon fell flat on his face.
Back through the fog, far, far west we go,
The tale of the dragon disappears from mind,
But who was the boy?
I'll leave you to find out.

Daniel Kinder (10)
Greenbank School

SPRING

Spring is finally here
Oh what a cheer.
The days are getting longer
So Dad's having a cool beer.
The bulbs are growing in the garden
And that looks just fine.
Mum's happy about that and has a glass of wine.
The kids chase the birds for a joke,
After an ice cold Coke.
This is the end of the season
The buds are finally open.
Oh I cannot wait 'til next spring.

Christina Maple (9)
Greenbank School

THE MAGICAL GARDEN

Can you hear the rustle of the leaves?
The greens are rich and beautiful,
The flowers glisten in all different colours,
The tall trees rise so high.
The variety of the garden is immense,
Little fairies and elves play in the leaves,
It is never the same in the garden,
One minute grey, the next flooded with greens,
Purples, pink.
This is my dream,
My favourite dream.

Rosamund Woodroffe (9)
Greenbank School

BONFIRE NIGHT

At last it is the fifth of November,
Having a bonfire in the back garden,
Guy Fawkes, Catherine wheels, Roman candles
And big rockets ready to *explode.*
Sparklers to whiz round and round
Like a Catherine wheel.
The Guy on the fire
Melting and melting
And it's been burnt.
The bonfire is over
So I have to wait a whole year
For the next bonfire night.

Adam Johnson (9)
Greenbank School

THE SPACESHIP

Orbiting the earth,
Going at 20,000km per hour,
America, South Africa, Tristan da Cunha,
I can see them all,
Earth, the little one,
Speeding through space,
Round and round the sun,
I've just seen the moon,
Suddenly I fly back into my seat,
I see flames as I re-enter the atmosphere,
Suddenly I jolt.
As we hit the ground we slow down,
While people come to meet us,
We think of what happened.

Tristan Honeyborne (9)
Greenbank School

BONFIRE

The bonfire roars,
Like slamming doors,
Flashing light,
Golden and bright,
Red and orange flames,
Just like it's all games,
That terrible night,
Oh! What a fright.

Sarah Gunning (9)
Greenbank School

Wintry Days

Choc-chip cakes,
Snowflakes,
Garden hose,
Red nose,
Hot tea,
How cold are we,
There's a white bush,
Here's some slush,
Fizzy pop,
Snowdrop.

Daniel Brown (8)
Greenbank School

RAIN

Rain looks like tears from a sad cloud,
Or it can look like sparkling diamonds
Falling from the heavens.
Rain looks like a shower of shimmering crystal,
Rain sounds like cans clattering on the floor
And the windows.
Sometimes rain can feel freezing cold
But sometimes it can feel boiling hot.
Rain can taste very refreshing.
Sometimes I wake up and hope it's a sunny day
To bring happiness and pleasure,
But sometimes rain can bring a lot more happiness
And pleasure than the sun.

Abigail Palmer (8)
Greenbank School

THE RAIN

I look out of the window
I see the rain pouring down on the trees
Splish splash
It reminds me of people crying
Very sad
Clattering and pattering
Dripping off the gutter.

Georgina McSorley (8)
Greenbank School

RAIN

Rain is like the sky crying,
It's just as if the sky is dying.
It smells like fish straight from the sea,
let's play outside, just you and me.
When it drops it clatters and crashes,
and along the windows it bashes.
Rain reminds me of ice and dull days,
it can be different in many ways.
When it rains it's really glum,
and you can't do anything,
It's not much fun!

Nina Rawlings (9)
Greenbank School

RAIN

I woke up in the morning
And look out the window,
What do I see?

I see rain, rain spitting down
The windowpane.
It is dull and black,
I will be bored again,
I wish it was sunny today.
It is very faint like diamonds falling,
People crying, it's a pain,
It feels like little stabs
Coming into me,
I wish it was sunny again.

Zoe Wildig (8)
Greenbank School

RAIN

Throwing rain into my face,
Get a coat it's raining again,
Splashing about with my friends,
Having lots of fun,
Getting dirty as can be,
Diamonds clattering into glass,
Tapping, splashing,
Coming down like people don't care,
I just love the rain,
I can't wait until the rain comes again.

Paul Exton-McGuinness (8)
Greenbank School

THE RAINBOW'S JOB

The rainbow's job's the hardest if you ask me,
One minute on land and the other on sea.

The rainbow wears to work each day,
Red of the apple,
Orange of the blazing fire,
Yellow of the daffodil,
Green of young grass,
Blue of an ocean,
Indigo of the deepest water,
Violet of the lavender,

The rainbow I would like to be,
As you travel from land to sea,
The rainbow, a friend of the bumblebee,
Leaves gold at the end of the line for me.

Sam Puttick (8)
Greenbank School

Rain

The rain sounds like clattering
Diamonds falling from the sky
It is beautiful
It looks like there are floods coming
It is refreshing, so refreshing
I rush outside
I have a shower,
A big long shower in the rain
It comes up to my knees
It is mixing up with the mud
Down by the river
It is rushing by
The fish are diving through the waves
They're so happy
It smells like fish, it smells like mustard
I play Pooh-sticks too.

Alexandra Dalton (8)
Greenbank School

COLOURS OF THE RAINBOW

Red   of the falling apples,
Orange of the beautiful sunset,
Yellow of the blazing sun,
Green   leaves on the beautiful trees,
Blue   of the bright sky we see,
Indigo of the deep blue sea,
Violet   of the smiling pansies,
         Mixed in a beautiful
                   rainbow.

James Bagnall (8)
Greenbank School

WINTER

W atery ice, glistening icicles like stalactites

I ce, bitterly cold, a blanket of cool snow

N ow snow covers fir trees,
       the prickles don't spike so much.
T orrential jump on a snowboard, a decent trick on skis
       and a perfect slide on a sleigh,
E verlasting fun having snowball fights
       and building brilliant snowmen!
R aindrops are coming again, now finally it's spring.

Andrew Goddard (8)
Greenbank School

WINTER

W inter snow coming down, cold as ice,
        landing on the ground like a feather.
I   n winter Jack Frost is about, going around
        making snow.
N o one can see him but he is about.

T iny bits of snow fall making a big blanket,

E veryone throwing snowballs, having lots of fun,

R unning around in warm, woolly clothes
        having lots of fun.
        Winter is nearly over, summer is beginning.

Natasha Phillips (8)
Greenbank School

RAIN

Rain is wet as the sea,
Rain is diamonds falling from the sky,
Rain is horses' hooves clattering on the ground,
Rain is see-through bouncy balls,
Rain is freckles on a face,
Rain is beautiful.

Joe Bacon (8)
Greenbank School

RAIN

As the rain comes clattering down
I wonder what it is
Giants' tears of diamonds and crystals
Maybe bongo drums
I will never know
But it's refreshing though
It tastes like salt
Thunder storms, puddles and water
It all comes from rain
Rain for hail and rain from buckets
Shaped like bullets.

Lewis Clarke (8)
Greenbank School

THE RAINBOW

Red of the robin's chest,
Orange of the sunsets,
Yellow of the smooth, soft sand,
Green of the tasty apples,
Blue of deep blue seas,
Indigo of the ink on the page,
That beautiful arch in front of the sea,
Violet pansies going swish in the air,
That wonderful bridge looking at me.

Thomas Theobold (9)
Greenbank School

RAIN

Water crystals banging on roofs,
Pouring down like showers,
Grass rises,
Seas are gushing,
Water refreshing in your face,
Grass damp,
Pitter-patter on the window sill,
A big rainbow appears
As the sun comes out.

Guy Hopkinson (8)
Greenbank School

RAIN

Rain, rain, it rains cats and dogs,
Heavy, dirty, cold, wet and dull,
Lots of ways the rain can be,
It clatters and bounces
When it hits the ground,
Rain, rain, lovely rain,
It makes puddles to splash in,
Rain can make floods
But it's fun to play in.

Tim Wrinch (8)
Greenbank School

WAR!

I stood in our house,
Quiet, like a mouse,
Mother, father,
Sister, brother,
The German planes,
Were as loud as diesel trains.

The bombs fell like rain,
People suffered the pain,
My heart was throbbing,
Whilst the bombs were dropping,
Babies crying,
People dying,
Devastation ran through the city,
People trapped, what a pity.
Flames rising into the sky,
We realised hell had arrived.
People suffering,
Buildings crumbling.

Mother, father trapped inside,
Sister, brother had died.
I buried my face in my knees,
Whilst the soot and dust were swept away
By a gentle breeze.

Charles Fair (10)
Greenbank School

EVACUATION

Mothers crying, sad to see their children go
Where they are going they do not know
All they know is they're off to the countryside
With a billeting officer by their side.

They climb on the train, often for the first time
Wondering where will I go?
Will the people be kind?
What will it be like?
Will I like the people I meet?
Will it be cosy with a fire at my feet?
Will I see things I've not see before?
Well except for in pictures, books and more.
After all these nice thoughts they could be wrong,
But I'll keep wondering for the journey's so long.

We arrive on the platform with a tag on our case,
All wondering what king of a future we face.
Before us are faces quite unfamiliar
All have something in common - something similar
They smile for a moment whilst each working out
Which one to take home, concealing their doubt.

I see a woman with long fair hair
She smiles and says 'May I have her over there?'
She comes towards me with a welcoming smile
And says 'Come along we'll be home in a while.'
My eyes start to water I can tell she'll be nice
But without my mum my heart feels like ice.

Hannah Bellamy (10)
Greenbank School

WAR!

War has come,
Dad's gone away,
Now it's time for me to say goodbye.
The billeting officer is here,
Mum's drowning in her tears.
On the way to my new home,
Big bombed buildings
Are scattered on the road.
I am here at my new home,
The person I'm living with
Is quite, quite old.
I look out of my window
It's pitch-black outside
In the distance I can see something
Light up the sky.
Wake up, wake up, I can hear,
The air raid warden's just been here.
After a pull out of bed I run downstairs
But to my horror a bomb fell somewhere
Crash, boom, crash boom,
The house had fallen down.
Crash, boom, crash, boom, crash.
The sound of a bell makes me cry,
My mum has sadly died.

Laura McSorley (10)
Greenbank School

BOMBING

Buildings have been coming down
The sound is loud all around
The people are really afraid
The bombs are coming down like rain.
Because of the air-raid
Hardly anyone has been saved
Loads and loads are lying dead
Whilst all the others have fled.

Jenna Perrin (10)
Greenbank School

WAR POEM

Children boarding trains,
Mothers crying on the platform,
Children screaming for their parents.

Children holding their toys,
With gas masks round their necks,
Billeting officers boarding trains
With their smart clothes.

'Start the engine,' shouts the driver,
The train slowly leaves the platform,
Evacuation has begun.

Myles Johnstone (10)
Greenbank School

EVACUATION

Children evacuated to a protected place,
Others have to stand and face,
The bombs are raining down and
Destroying everything in sight,
Every day and every night,
What will my new home be like?
Will it have toys, games or a bike?
I dream that I see my parents again,
While I sit with other children on the train.

William Mitchell (11)
Greenbank School

WAR!

War has come,
Banging from a gun,
Killing people here and there,
Blood streaming everywhere.

Men are going away,
Missing families every day,
Women are taking their place,
As soldiers retreat to their base.

In rationing there's not enough,
Families finding it quite tough.
Shortages here and there,
Now mostly everywhere.

Almost the end of the war,
Spirits are quite low.
People have been stranded everywhere,
Not knowing where to go.

Jessica McGeorge (10)
Greenbank School

Women's War Work

Every night I patrol the street,
Making sure there are no lights.
Scared I hurry on.
Wishing there were no bombs that are
Going to drop and kill everyone.
As I walk across the fields,
Everything is new to me.
Since the war has started,
Men have gone to war.
I have joined the Land Army.
A fire blazing in front of me,
The fireman call to me to get the hose ready
To put out the fire.
A woman screaming for her child,
The child tearful and afraid
Because of the air raid.

Sarah Cottis (10)
Greenbank School

BLITZ

The alarm was raised twenty minutes before,
I felt scared, very scared.
My mum and I rushed to the shelter,
The shelter was packed with the ill,
Old people and whining babies.
There came a rumble,
Dogs barked and babies screamed,
There was a burst of heat,
Bangs and crackles like fireworks,
Then silence.

Andrew Ford (10)
Greenbank School

INDEPENDENT WOMEN

As their husbands and children pass
before their eyes,
The women have to be strong.
They don't know whether
they will ever see their loved ones again,
For their families and friends could be in pain
at any time while they are at war,
For their husbands and sons have gone to war,
and their children are living far away,
in somebody else's home.
The Germans will pay for all
the hurt and distress caused.
Everyone is sad, weeping,
having so much woe and sorrow.
The women have to work instead of the men,
they have to serve their term during the war.
The women must hold on and so must everyone
at least until the war has gone!

Sara Shimi (10)
Greenbank School

AIR RAID

All was silent for most of the night,
Until the planes started to fight,
Everyone running for the bomb shelters,
Seeing their homes crumbling to pieces,
Bullets flying through the air.
Skimming over everywhere,
People dying everywhere
Children evacuated to the country
Boys and girls are full of pity
Missing their parents in the city,
Planes flying and bombing Dover.
I hope the war will soon be over.

Richard Kemp (11)
Greenbank School

LEARNING

Teachers try to make you learn,
but all you do is sit and burn.
At first maths seems great,
but then you realise and start to hate.
English may seem good,
but then you turn and hide in your hood.
At the start science seems so nice,
but then you start to hide like mice.
History may seem okay,
but suddenly you feel like you want to play.
Maybe spelling workshop looks all right,
then you feel as you've been beaten by a knight.
Handwriting seems fine,
suddenly it's looking like it's not mine.
Wonderful is RE,
but then you want to do PE.
Terrible may be all the work,
but I know I won't be a twerp.

Michael Edge (9)
Hursthead Junior School

DOGS

Newfoundlands are slow and slobber,
Labradors are fast and fidgety,
Terriers are pests and are passionate,
Sausage dogs are long and loud,
Spaniels are strong and strokeable,
Setters are thin and tail-wagging,
Rottweilers are small and smelly,
Dalamatians are spotty and sensitive.

Remember dogs are for life not just for Christmas!

Megan Biggar (10)
Hursthead Junior School

My Dad

My dad is clever, he wants to go on Millionaire
Trouble is he's unfashionable with his brown spiky hair
He makes us all laugh, he is so funny and kind
But makes us all scowl with his smelly behind
He's always so silly and chases us around
He really is the best dad around.

Lauren Gill (9)
Hursthead Junior School

WHAT DOES MY CAT DO ALL DAY?

What does my cat do all day?
Does she sit and play?

What does she do when I'm at school?
Does she play in the pool?

Does she play with friends?
Maybe at the weekend?

Do cats go to school?
Is that why they're cool?

What does my cat do all day?
Does she sit and play?

I don't know, I'm afraid to say
I'll try and find out another day.

Jennifer King (9)
Hursthead Junior School

A Daily Run Of My Brother, Philip

At breakfast my brother, Phil, is messy eating his cereal,
He is very young and looks so small as he walks with me to school.
The teachers say he's chatty and sometimes funny too,
His blond hair gets wet as he splashes in the bath,
Soon after he is sleepy and ready for his bed,
I love him when he's sleeping, he's really, really
   Cute!

James Cresswell (8)
Hursthead Junior School

INSIDE THE . . .

Inside the box
You will find
A red rat running
A yellow yeti yelling
A blue bear boxing
A grey gopher golfing
A pink panda panting
Inside the box.

James Thornley (7)
Hursthead Junior School

My Budgie

My budgie is feathery
He is bluey-grey
His name is Max
He likes to relax.

Max is always in a happy mood
He loves to eat his budgie food
He pecks his swing with his beak
He does it all throughout the week.

Max dings his bell
And chirps loudly as well
He eats out of my hand
I say Max is the king of budgie land!

Verity Rushton (9)
Hursthead Junior School

DAD'S CAR

My dad's car keeps breaking down
It couldn't even get to town
It pops and bangs just like a gun
My dad says 'This is not fun.'

He saved his money and bought one new
It's got pop-up lights and is shiny blue
My dad's car is really ace
He drives it like he's in a race.

Robert Blease (9)
Hursthead Junior School

IMAGINE

Imagine a flower
As tall as a tower.

Imagine a pig
Wearing a wig.

Imagine a gale
Shift a whale.

Imagine your brain
Going insane.

But that's in my head,
I think I should stick with my bed!

Jack Moores (9)
Hursthead Junior School

MY DAD

I have a dad
Who is completely mad -
He plays tricks on us,
And drives a silver bus.

His eyes are brown,
On his forehead a frown.
His hair is wavy,
And the colour of gravy.

He has big clumpy feet,
And they don't smell so sweet!
But I'm just glad -
That he's *my dad!*

Rebecca Thomas (8)
Hursthead Junior School

BIONIC BILL

Bill has got eyes that can see through anything,
Bill can smell the scent of paper,
Bill can make us know any language,
Bill can kill with his laser finger,
Bill can grab with his twenty arms,
Bill runs as quick as light
Bill makes clanking and whirring noises
Guess what he is?
A robot!

Tristan Russell (9)
Hursthead Junior School

THE MINOTAUR

The minotaur tail rips round you and squeezes you
His sweating horns butt you against the rock wall
He kicks you to the stony ground and rips you over his shoulder
He twirls you in the air and you drop to the ground.

Charles Hartle (9)
Hursthead Junior School

WEIRD ANIMALS

I know a fish who's always cold,
So he wears a vest made of gold.
I know a bird who's scared of height,
So he walks always all day and all night.
I know a horse who cannot run,
So he bought a car and drove for fun.
I know a bat who couldn't see in the night,
So he carried a torch around for light.
I know an ant who lives on his own,
To speak to his friends he uses the phone.
None of these animals are the same,
But if they were it would be a shame.

Bethany Williams (9)
Hursthead Junior School

My Dad

My dad is tall and slim
With big blue eyes and a playful grin.
His hair is brown and thinning on top,
And when he's angry I think he might pop.
My dad is clever, he can make anything,
But one big problem, he can't even sing.
He loves his hi-fi and he likes it on *loud*
But one thing for sure, he makes me proud.
Because unlike all the rest,
My dad is the *best!*
(Even though he's fifty)

Adam Crowder (8)
Hursthead Junior School

AT THE SEASIDE

It's warm today,
Let's go and play
'To the beach,' said Mum
Let's hope for some sun.

The beach is busy,
Everybody is having fun.
Splashing in the sea,
Enjoying the sun.

Let's play ball on the sand,
Everybody running together, hand in hand,
Screaming and shouting like the noise of a band
It's fun playing down on the sand.

Olivia McGahey (8)
Hursthead Junior School

THE CITY

When I go in the city, I see parks that are pretty.
Litter thrown in the street, which gets caught around people's feet.
The tramp huddles in a corner, I hope he can get a bit warmer.
I look up in the sky, the buildings are so high,
I see the pigeons resting on the gutters,
I wish it wasn't so noisy and cluttered.

Charlie Amos-Brown (8)
Hursthead Junior School

THE TIGER

The tiger wakes up and steps out from his den,
He washes himself and roars and then . . .
He goes out hunting, to try to catch his tea,
Hopefully he'll see a deer and won't get *me*!
Aaaghh!

Stephanie Lee (8)
Hursthead Junior School

CITY

It's busy, people running all around
Bumping and bouncing
Traffic jams here and there, almost everywhere.
People getting takeaways
And going to work each day.
Never talking, just keep on walking
As the day goes by.
The day is gone, the night is here
So go to bed my dear.

Becky Dawson (9)
Hursthead Junior School

MY DAD

My dad is tall, he absolutely loves football.
My dad supports City, when they lose it's a pity.
When they score, there's such a big roar!
My dad's great, he's my best mate.
My dad likes to have a jog, but he won't let us have a dog.
My dad's nickname is Sim
And he's my dad and I love him!

Sophie Fletcher (9)
Hursthead Junior School

MY DAD

My dad's hair is red and wavy,
He wears dark blue jeans
On his very long legs.
His voice is deep and very well heard
He also is very happy when my team have won a match.
His T-shirt is dark blue
And has a City sign on it.
My dad's favourite team is Manchester City
His hobby is doing work in Stockport
Whatever my dad does he's the best.

Chris Russell (8)
Hursthead Junior School

My Uncle Rob

My uncle Rob is the tallest man I've ever seen,
My uncle Rob is so jolly.
He's sillier than his dog Molly.
With bushy hair you've never seen,
Long black hair on his chest.
He's very bright
And sometimes just sometimes,
He's very, very comforting.

Oliver Bristow (9)
Hursthead Junior School

POSH PIG

On yonder farm there lived a pig
Wearing a very stylish wig
A modelling career he thought he'd choose
So he went out and bought lots of shoes
High heels, low heels, no heels at all
He had to be careful he didn't fall
His long, pink ears and his great big snout
He would be a model without a doubt.

Nicola Macleod (8)
Hursthead Junior School

MY DOG

My dog is called Shadow,
He is golden and fair,
When I am sad,
He is always there.

He is my best friend,
I love him to bits,
He lies and begs,
And stands and sits.

I take him for walks,
By streams and rivers,
He gets very wet,
And shakes and shivers.

He will shake my hand,
And stay by my door,
He's my big buddy,
For evermore!

Elizabeth Bateman (9)
Hursthead Junior School

THE WHITE DAY

It has snowed all day
And the ground's all white.
I can't wait to go outside
But it's just not fair.
I can't get out
The window's stuck with ice
I stand looking through my window
At such a splendid sight.
But I don't care
I'm in here
Where it's lovely, dry and bright.

Adam Ramsden-Smith (8)
Hursthead Junior School

MY DAD

My dad has enormous feet
But apart from that, he's really sweet.
He's very cuddly and always funny
But I'm not going to tell you about the size of his tummy.
His hair is black, but there's very little of that
So he usually wears a warm, fleecy hat.

Anna Louise Peate (8)
Hursthead Junior School

MARS TO THE STARS

When me and space,
Came face to face,
A long, long time ago,
Oh, what a shock I had to see,
The Earth so far below.

But when I looked into the sky,
Gazing at planets, so high, so high,
Mercury, Venus, Neptune and Mars
Surrounded by millions of twinkling stars.

Hayley Ramsden (8)
Hursthead Junior School

WHAT A WONDERFUL PLACE

Sea and land
What a wonderful place.
Plants and nature
What a beautiful place.
With sun and moon
What a mysterious place.
Sky and ground
What a gigantic place.
Homes to live in
What a snuggly place.
With friends and family
What a happy place.
Lots to play with, lots to do
What an exciting place.
With schools to learn in
What an inspiring place.
Beds to sleep in, chairs to sit on
What a comfortable place.
With music to listen to
What a relaxing place.
Guess where this wonderful place is . . .
Earth!

Sam Roe (8)
Hursthead Junior School

KATE'S PETS

In her bedroom Kate kept . . .
Ten swimming fish
Nine grunting pigs
Eight singing birds
Seven woofing dogs,
Six buzzing bees
Five croaking frogs
Four mooing cows
Three squeaking mice
Two hissing snakes
And one guess what?
Lion!

Kate Earnshaw (9)
Hursthead Junior School

DINOSAURS

D angerous
I ncredible
N asty
O bjectionable
S tomping
A ggressive
U gly
R oaring
S cary . . .

Benjamin Devereux (9)
Hursthead Junior School

ANIMALS

Wouldn't we all like to have a pet
Like a cat to stroke whilst it sleeps
Or a dog we walk in the park
These are just two of my favourite pets.

I would like a horse
A small and brown one would be nice
I could ride it on a country lane
And see the wildlife all around.

I wouldn't like to own a frog
It's horrible and slimy
And cold and wet
It jumps around and makes a horrible sound.

I wouldn't like a rat either
It's dirty and smelly
It carries lots of germs
And it moves fast and silent.

My favourite animal is an elephant
I like to see them in the water
They blow water from their trunks
And they are big and strong.

Sophie Dyde (8)
Hursthead Junior School

TRAIN ON THE TRACK

Clickety-clack, train on the track,
Going around the turntable.
Clickety-clack, train on the track,
Stopping for coal and water.
Clickety-clack, train on the track,
Fireman turning on the water tap.
Clickety-clack, train on the track,
Stopping at the station.
Clickety-clack, train on the track,
Driver is frying eggs and bacon.
Clickety-clack, train on the track,
Guard blows his whistle.
Clickety-clack, train on the track,
Climbing up the hill to the mill.
Clickety-clack, train on the track,
Gathering speed down the hill.
Clickety-clack, train on the track,
Zooming around the corners.
Clickety-clack, train on the track,
Happy passengers reading papers.
Clickety-clack, my name's Jack,
And I want to drive this train on the track.

Jack Green (8)
Hursthead Junior School

CRAZY SCHOOL!

Paper planes soaring
Lessons boring
Silent reading
Still proceeding
Can't wait till home time
It's only half past nine
Playtime is over
Our teacher Ms Rover.

Stand in line
Dinner time
Eat up quick and
Out to play
It's the middle
Of the day.

3 o'clock
Nearly home time
Collect the reading book of mine
10 past 3, 5 minutes to go
Oh why do school days go so slow?
Homework done, free at last
Why do evenings go so fast?
Put to bed at 5 to 9
Wonder when I'll be back in line?

Matthew Oates (9)
Hursthead Junior School

MY DAD

My dad is kind
My dad is great
On Saturday night he lets me stay up late.
My dad is tall and very slim
And when he's happy he makes me grin.
His hair is short and going grey,
He always has a lot to say.
I think my dad is best of all
Because he's the one who knows it all.

Philip Moorhouse (9)
Hursthead Junior School

An Alien Comes To Stay

An alien came to stay one day
He was from the planet Mars,
He had 4 eyes and antennaes
And he didn't half run fast!
He was lots of fun to play with,
And people stopped to stare,
With his purple hands and his purple feet
And his purple, spiky hair.

Matthew Drury (8)
Hursthead Junior School

MY BROTHERS

My brother Dan,
Likes to eat ham,
And it makes him go hyper all day.

But my other brother Rob,
Is as lazy as a frog,
And he's really, really funny like me.

They think they're really cool,
But they're just big fools,
And there's nothing else that you can say!

Emma Taylor (8)
Hursthead Junior School

MY GRANDPA

My grandpa is the kindest man
He's tall and big and I'm his greatest fan
He has a tickly moustache that's grey
And always lets us go to play
He's happy and kind and really silly
And has such a funny name that's
. . . Billy!

Amie Thompson (9)
Hursthead Junior School

TELEVISION

I like Kenan, I like Kel,
But I think they truly smell.
I watch wrestling, I think it's tough,
I like movies I can't get enough.
I like videos on the spot,
Some are OK and some are top.
My favourite movies are action-packed,
I hate the ones that are actual fact.

Patrick Whitehead (9)
Hursthead Junior School

THE FRIENDLY PENGUIN

I'm the friendly penguin,
I'd like to say 'Hello,'
But my bottom's getting cold,
'Cause I'm sitting in the snow!

I'm the friendly penguin,
I'll say 'How do you do?'
I'll have a few fishes please,
Just one or two.

I'm the friendly penguin,
I think I'll have to go home,
Because at the moment,
I'm all alone.

I'm the friendly penguin,
I'll have to say 'Bye-bye,'
I'm going to miss you,
I think I'll cry.

Chloe Dowdle (8)
Hursthead Junior School

I WISH, I WISH

Mum please, oh Mum
Will you let me have a dog?
They're furry and cute and loveable
Oh I wish I had one.

Mum, oh please, oh Mum
Can I have another hamster?
They're fast and furious
And they nibble you when you give them food.

Mum please, oh Mum
Can I have another fish?
I know what kind it will be like,
Spotty, orange, red and black.
Thanks Mum!

Clare Heap (8)
Hursthead Junior School

MY GRANDPA

My grandpa is tall, his hair is grey,
He lets us go round to his house and play.
He thinks he's funny, and has a loud laugh,
But I just look because he's always daft.
My grandpa is chatty and very loud,
But when I'm with him, I'm very proud.

Katie Thompson (9)
Hursthead Junior School

MY FAMILY

There's five in my family and that's including me,
There's my brother who is eleven
And my sister who is seven
There's my dad who's thirty-six
And my mum is too,
My brother's got a small room
Which is going to be decorated really soon
My room is big and long
I think as big as Hong Kong
My mum's and dad's room is normal size
And that's because they are wise
My sister's room is normal too
And it smells brand new!

Daniel Newman (8)
Hursthead Junior School

WHY?

Who do all the bees fly?
Why do clouds stay up in the sky?
Why?
Why do rubber balls bounce?
Why do growling tigers pounce?
Why?
Why do birds fly away?
Why do horses feed on hay?
Why?
Why does life go on and on?
Why do mirrors reflect the sun?
Why?
Why is wood used for many things?
Why do wasps give you their stings?
Why?
Why do people joke about?
Why do babies scream and shout?
Why?
Why are people not the same?
Why are some animals not as tame?
Why?
Why does the world go round and round?
Why do some creatures not make a sound?
Why?
Why does God do all these things?
Why is it messages that he brings?
Why?
Why?

Georgina Lunt (9)
Hursthead Junior School

FIRE

Fire blazing as hot as steel,
Swords of flame dancing in a lava pool
Burning through forests, like a rat through a drain,
Scaring the people, going insane.

The smoke is grey, choking the air
As the flames die out and move elsewhere.
Shattered ruins, the land is deserted,
Flowers and trees soon to please.

Patrick Bucknall (8)
Hursthead Junior School

FOOTBALL CRAZY

Football games are the best
They are better than all the rest

Man United are my team
They are really, really supreme

There's Cole, Keane and Beckham too
Who are some of the players who get the team through

They've won the cup so many times
And did the treble in 'Ninety Nine'

What is left for such a team?
Who have realised their every dream

The City fans must sometimes say
'Why can't we see that kind of play?'

Luke Burras (8)
Hursthead Junior School

MY UNCLE NEIL

Uncle Neil he's so sporty,
And at times he's very naughty.
He plays the guitar in a musical way,
But often very loud!
He is a teacher, he is very clever,
Some say he's silly, we say never.
He plays with us when it is sunny,
And he is often very funny.

John Russ (8)
Hursthead Junior School

MY COUSIN JACK

My cousin Jack is bouncy and bright
He'd keep you up on the darkest night
My cousin Jack dresses to be tough
But ends up looking dirty and rough
Sometimes he is very mean
But he is quite funny, when he licks the plate clean
But I don't care what he's like
He's my cousin Jack, that's all I mind.

Charley Moore (8)
Hursthead Junior School

FOUL FOOTBALL

I run to the goal with the ball
I get kicked in the leg
And I fall
Penalty kick
I feel sick
I shoot
Kicking with my brand new boots
Goal!

Stephen Lyons (8)
Hursthead Junior School

A MYSTERY PET

Let me tell you about this pet,
Its fur is soft, its nose is wet.
Its floppy ears are very long,
In the jungle it doesn't belong.
It has a fluffy tail,
And it isn't a snail.
It eats lettuce and carrots,
And it's not a parrot.
It might be a dog,
But it's definitely not a frog.
It's not necessarily a cat,
It can't be a rat.
Is it a cow? Is it a horse?
No, it's not; it's a rabbit of course!

Gemma Lakin (8)
Hursthead Junior School

A Rainy Day

Plop, plop,
Drop, drop,
Goes the rain
It's another rainy day
So I have to stay in
I can't go anywhere
I don't think it's fair
Bang! Bang!
Goes the rain on the dustbin
It's another rainy day.

James Bishop (9)
Hursthead Junior School

GINA THE GIRAFFE

Tall and elegant
Long and lean
Gina giraffe
She's the Jungle Queen.

Her neck goes down
A thin, straight line
Gina the giraffe
She looks so fine.

She runs like the wind
She smiles like the sun
Gina giraffe
Just loves to have fun!

Moya Kerr (9)
Hursthead Junior School

SPACE

Space, pitch black
Nothing to see,
Stars shining bright,
The moon, a white light.

Space, never ending,
Comets and shooting stars
The planets in our solar system,
Earth, Jupiter, Saturn and Mars.

Space for everyone to see
Space a total mystery!

Philip Kent (9)
Hursthead Junior School

THE TALE OF A ROMAN SOLDIER

There was a Roman soldier
His name was Jimmy Hall
And he'd been a bit naughty
So he was sent to Hadrian's Wall.

It was very, very windy
And very cold at nights
He missed the Coliseum
And the gladiator fights.

Then he saw some Scotsmen
They didn't like each other
So Jimmy took a shot at them
With his Onega.

They all ran away
And didn't dare come back
His friends said Jimmy's a hero
He gave those Scots a whack.

He said to the Centurion
'Look how well I've done
Can I go home now
And see what's going on.'

The Centurion said to Jimmy
'You can go back to Italy
And when you get there
You can have a pizza for tea.'

Nick Delap (8)
Hursthead Junior School

NIGHT-TIME

Every night when I go to bed
I dream of many things.
Of things to do and things to be
And things that make me scream.
My duvet is a monster,
My pillows they are ghosts
So when morning finally comes around
I'm glad it's just a dream.
But sometimes nights are different,
I dream of special things
Like who to be when I am grown
And tall and strong and brave.
One night I'm a football player
I'm playing in the Cup
The whistle blows, the cheers begin
And I score the final goal!
But dreams are only ever dreams
And morning always comes
So whether I had nightmares
Or whether I had dreams
If the day is any weekday
I know I'll be off to school.

Thomas Mortimer (8)
Hursthead Junior School

WEIRD WEATHER

Rain rushing down the road
Quick, wrap up it's getting cold
Snow swirling through the sky
A beautiful breeze blowing by.
Hurricanes howling high and low
Freezing frost, can't feel my toe
Misty morning, moist and wet
Shining sun scorching, what a bet!
Hail heavy and hops up and down
Twirling twister, where's my gown?
Thunder thrashing like a bomb.

Elizabeth Henshall (9)
Hursthead Junior School

My Dad

My dad whose name is Howard
Is always brave and not a coward.
His voice is very strong and loud
Especially in a football crowd.
His hair is brown, his eyes are blue
He's very clever and funny too.

Colin Lees (8)
Hursthead Junior School

MY DAD

My dad reads a golf book,
But has never learned to cook . . .
He has a big mind,
And is really kind.
He hogs the computer,
And doesn't like a scooter.

He watches sports,
And wears orange shorts.
He has a grey car,
That drives really far.
But my dad's the best,
And beats all the rest.

Michael Orton (9)
Hursthead Junior School

ANIMALS

Animals are small
Animals are big
Animals are yellow
Pink white and green
Animals are fast
Animals are slow
Animals are tall
Animals are short
Animals are go, go, go.

Alex Fripp (9)
Hursthead Junior School

FRIENDS

Being friends is very important.
Some people have best friends,
Some people just have friends,
My best friend is called Becky.

Becky is a friend of mine,
We play together most of the time.
Sometimes we disagree,
But we always make up and say sorry.

On nice sunny days we play on our bikes,
On windy days we may fly our kites.
On cloudy days we stay at home,
Dress up, play music and talk on the phone.

Me and Becky are friends all the time,
Sometimes we act as though we are on cloud nine.

My friend Becky is my very important best friend.

Maria Redfern (9)
Hursthead Junior School

PAT'S PETS

In her bedroom Pat keeps
10 dolphins in her bed
9 elephants in her drawer
8 monkeys in her plant
7 dogs in her wardrobe
6 cats in her light
5 rats in her dress
4 mice in her skirt
3 rabbits in her knickers
2 slugs in her slippers, and
1 . . . in her vest, guess what?
A wallaby!
Ha, ha, ha, ha!

Jade Galtrey-Smith
Hursthead Junior School

My Dad

My dad is really funny,
He loves it bright and sunny.
He's really clever and witty,
And works hard in the centre of the city.
He enjoys a drop of whisky,
But he won't do anything risky.
He knows a lot about IT,
That's all about computers, you see.
His favourite team is Liverpool,
You can't blame him; they're so cool.
His favourite food is curry and rice,
He really enjoys all that spice.
After school he joined the Navy,
But missed his mum's roast chicken and gravy.
He loves my mum so dearly,
You can see that very clearly.
His birthday is on Valentine's Day,
Which means that tomorrow it's coming his way.
All in all my dad's the best,
He is better than all the rest.

Francesca Miller (8)
Hursthead Junior School

POETIC VOYAGES

Red is like an angry face
Orange is like the food we eat.
Yellow is like hot sand
Green is like a buttercup meadow
Blue is like a shiny wave
Purple is like a juicy plum
Indigo is like a lovely night sky
Violet is like the pretty bluebells.

Elaina Mirams (8)
Hursthead Junior School

POETIC VOYAGES

Inside the . . .
Inside the box
You will find
A yellow yeti yawning
A red rat rocking
A brown bear baying
A pink panda pouncing
A white whale wailing
Inside the box
Inside the box.

Sam Ormrod (8)
Hursthead Junior School

Dogs

Dogs are furry
Dogs are playful
Dogs are cute
Dogs are good at eating
Dogs are small
Dogs are fast
Dogs are big
Dogs are loud
Dogs like bones
Dogs are happy
Dogs are like a ball of fluff.

Adam Ogdon (7)
Hursthead Junior School

POETIC VOYAGES

Red is like an angry face,
Orange is like an orange top,
Yellow is like a yellow sun,
Green is like the grass swaying,
Blue is like a bluebird flying,
Purple is like a purple hair band,
Violet is like a violet bracelet,
Indigo is like an indigo necklace.

Charlotte Bruton (8)
Hursthead Junior School

POETIC VOYAGES

Inside the . . .
Inside the box
You will find
A red, rushing rhubarb
An orange ostrich overtaking
A silver snake slithering
A bluebird burping
A yellow yak yacking
Inside the box
Inside the box.

Zoe Allen (7)
Hursthead Junior School

Poetic Voyages

Red is like an angry face
Orange is like an octopus
Yellow is like a yowling yackle
Green is like a growling grasshopper
Blue is like a bouncing badger
Indigo is like an insect ignoring
Lilac is like a leaping lion
Silver is like a snake sliding.

Hannah Woods (7)
Hursthead Junior School

INSIDE THE BOX

Inside the . . .
Inside the box
You will find
A red rabbit running
An orange owl hooting
A blue badger baying
A golden goose gaggling
A purple panda patting
Inside the box
Inside the box.

Robin Helsby (7)
Hursthead Junior School

IF I WERE . . .

If I were a spider, I would bite,
If I were a snail, I would slide in the night.
If I were a worm, I would wriggle and wiggle,
If I were an ant, I would tickle your middle.
If I were a grasshopper, I would jump very high,
If I were a ladybird, I would make myself fly.

Callum Moughan (8)
Hursthead Junior School

In The Box

In the box there is a red rabbit running
In the box there is a great giraffe galloping
In the box there is a weird witch winking
In the box there is a big, bad bug bowing
In the box there is a green grasshopper grinning
In the box there is a ginormous giant joking.

Daniel Gurney (7)
Hursthead Junior School

POETIC VOYAGES

Inside the box
Inside the box
You will find
A red rat running
An orange octopus oozing
A blue bee bumbling
A yellow yak yacking
A purple panda peering
Inside the box
Inside the box.

Jessica Vallance (7)
Hursthead Junior School

POETIC VOYAGES

Inside the box
You will find
A pink panther running
A red rat sprinting
A purple rabbit racing
Inside the box
Inside the box.

Adam Martin (8)
Hursthead Junior School

POETIC VOYAGES

Animals are beautiful
Animals are yucky
Animals are cute but mostly lucky.

Animals go jumping around,
Animals are cute
Animals go here and there, except newts.

Daniel Wood (8)
Hursthead Junior School

POETIC VOYAGES

Inside the . . .
Inside the box
There is a red, racing fox
A yellow cheetah, cheating and eating
A big brown bear banging on bars
A green gorilla grinning
Inside the box
Inside the box.

Alex Law (7)
Hursthead Junior School

POETIC VOYAGES

If I were a yellow yak I would yowl all day
If I were a silver snake I would slither all day
If I were a beautiful butterfly I would blush all day
If I were a green grasshopper I would growl all day
If I were a mouldy mole I would munch all day
If I were a buzzy bee I would buzz like a badger all day.

Robert Gulson (8)
Hursthead Junior School

CATS AND DOGS

Cats are fat
Cats are furry
Cats are lovely
Cats are purry
Dogs are barky
Dogs are runny
Dogs are playful
Dogs are lucky.

James Mallalieu (8)
Hursthead Junior School

MY HOBBY

My hobby is rollerblading
It really is great fun
I speed-skate round the corners
And sometimes fall on my bum.
My mum sits in the cafe
Drinking tea and reading her book
As I skate past I shout to her
To come and have a look.
I skate round to the music
My favourite is 'Rock DJ'
Mum comes and says 'It's time to go
You can come back another day.'

Ben Porter (9)
Hursthead Junior School

My Dad

My daddy is called Andy,
He is sometimes very handy.
He has brown, curly hair,
That goes everywhere.
Cos he doesn't get it cut very often.
He wears the funniest, blue, fluffy jumper
You have ever seen
To the really nice shops,
He's never been.
But my dad is *happy* the way he is!

Laura Darroch (9)
Hursthead Junior School

MUM'S COOL

My mum is cool and plays in the pool
I help her cook as she reads the book
My mum is fun when she eats a cream bun
She gets in a mood when I'm rude
But I have fun with my mum all day in the sun.

Zoe Arshamian (8)
Hursthead Junior School

MY DAD

My dad is big and sweet
He always has smelly feet
Every day he stays in bed
Under the covers, you can't see his head
I love my dad so much
I don't know what I'd do without him!

Jack Worne (8)
Hursthead Junior School

MY TEACHER

I once had a teacher, Miss Fickter
She was attacked by a boa constrictor
She struggled, she fought
The snake she caught
In the face, with her handbag
Good sport.

She's also extremely tall
Unlike Miss Hadwart who's small
And I remember the day
When her hat blew away
Then she found it on Sunday.

Matthew Wood (8)
Hursthead Junior School

MY MAGIC BOX

I will put in my box,
the scent of a brand new pen that has just been opened,
and a lock of hair that has never been touched,
a newborn baby that is one second old,
and the tooth of a fully grown T-Rex.
I will put in my box,
all of the seven seas roaring like the biggest dragon
and all the big rainforests.

My box is made of shark skin, leaves off trees,
and grass with half frost.
I will keep my box under my bed,
tied down with a weight.

Thomas Deluce (8)
Lum Head Primary School

MY MAGIC BOX

In my box I will put
a photo of my family,
I will keep the capital of kindness,
and a photo of my cats.
I will keep the silk of butterflies,
the memory of a Welsh beach,
see a sunset,
hear a dolphin speak,
and see a puppy playing.

My box has dolphin skin on top
and a shark too
and lion skin on the corners.
The lock is made of gold, silver and bronze,
and one day I will fly to the Bahamas
for a day across the ocean.

Douglas Cragg (7)
Lum Head Primary School

MY MAGIC BOX

In my box I will put
The big, hot, burning sun,
The cold breeze everywhere
The angels in the heavens,
and the kittens feel like a silky blanket
The sound of the sea roaring,
and the sound of wobbly jelly.

In my box
Jupiter will turn small,
Pluto will be big
The sound of bones cracking,
and vines breaking
The taste of mouth-watering sweets
The taste of lollipops
The tiger's eyes peeling
The fluffy kitten lying in a million roses
and the moaning of my sister.

My box is made from
Icy cold raindrops
and snowflakes all over
and a glowing star for a key.

Nicole Driscoll (8)
Lum Head Primary School

MY MAGIC BOX

I will put in my box
the bright twinkle in my dad's eyes when he sees me
the sound of my mum's laughter.

In my box I will put
all of the letters I sent to my dad,
a key to a door that only true friends of mine
can find, the door that I sit behind.

My box is made of the fur of a Beanie Baby
Classic dog called Scooter.

Kelly Lynch (8)
Lum Head Primary School

Magic Box

I will put in my box
The shine of a spotless table
The blossom from a newborn tree
Ten babies screaming their heads off.

I will put in my box
The smell of an old, dead body,
A newborn kitten cuddled and hugged
Raindrops dropping from a roof.

I will put in my box
A freezing cold snowflake
The fragrance of a new perfume
The smell of a cold strawberry.

My box is made from air
Covered in twinkling stars
And the hinges are made from tigers' claws.

Christalla Towli (8)
Lum Head Primary School

MY MAGIC BOX

I will put in my box
the sound of footballers cheering
as they have just won
the bright, gleaming eyes of a cheetah,
the rustle of leaves on trees.

I will put in my box
the sound of the sea roaring in a storm,
the sound of a woodpecker going tic, tic, tic on a tree,
the sound of a kitten purring with joy on your knee.

My box is made from ice,
it's got icicles hanging from the bottom.
My box will take me across the seven seas.

Christopher Bergin (8)
Lum Head Primary School

MY MAGIC BOX

I will put in my box
The first feather to fall off a bird
The sea roaring, bringing sand to the shore
And a shell that will give me good luck
A multicoloured zebra eating ten song notes
I will pick the best bird that will sing to me at night.

I will put in my box
Three dolphins jumping in the sea, splashing water
Snowflakes falling from the sky,
An angel in my dream.

My box is made out of
Marble stones and red glitter all over it.

Rebekah Hughes (8)
Lum Head Primary School

MY MAGIC BOX

I will put in my box
A cheetah with scary eyes
I will put Jupiter and the sun burning with fire
In my box I will put a shiny, gold star
In my box I will put the wind rustling on my face
I will put in my box a shiny, gleaming pen
I will put in my box a new car that's just come out.
My box is made out of cheetah skin
And ice at the corners
At the top it has cheetah's skin.

Daanyal Naveed (7)
Lum Head Primary School

MY MAGIC BOX

I will put in my box
the waving sea
which looks like it's touching the sky
the taste of my cold lollipop.

I will put in my box
the touch of a gleaming star
the sparkle of an earring so bright.

I will put in my box
the blue and green of Earth from outer space
the yellow of Venus so hot.

I will put in my box
the first winter ever
the first planet of all the world.

My box is made from
gold and silver with a brass lock
I will keep my box in a room
where only two friends of mine
and me can come in.

Marie Gabriella Haastrup (7)
Lum Head Primary School

MY MAGIC BOX

In my box I will have
a waterfall with a drop
of crystal water in it.

The wind's warm breeze
blowing my top from side to side.

And the hot, dehydrating sun
shining in the beautiful, shining waterfall.

And the shine of a cat's eyes
with a little sparkling dazzle.

Josh Lincoln (8)
Lum Head Primary School

MY MAGIC BOX

I will put in my box
the soft feel of silky roses
the sound of the sea
sparkly stars floating in the sky.

I will put in my box
the scent of flowers
autumn leaves blowing in my face
the sound of a lake rippling.

I will put in my box
the first day of spring
the sound of the birds' song
the sound of the Amazon rainforest.

I will put in my box
a sparkly falling star
the taste of a passionate coconut.

My box is made of
Multicoloured glitter with a gold lock
and an invisible key
I will fly on my box and land on gems.

Anber Jamal (8)
Lum Head Primary School

MY MAGIC BOX

I will put in my box
the sound of popstar's singing
and my mum's sparkling party earrings
the gleaming stars that sparkle at night
and a photo of my family
and the smiles of cousins and aunts and uncles.

I will put in my box
all the video games I can think of
and the crayons that keep me occupied.

My box is made out of diamonds and crystals
but don't touch it, it's spiky.
I keep my box under the creaky floorboards
the key is at the side
and whenever I open my box
the wind blows in my face like outside.

Safa Milad (8)
Lum Head Primary School

MY MAGIC BOX

I will put in my box
the swish of the waves in the sea
the touch of the walls in the houses
the breeze of the freezer ice.

I will put in my box
the rustling of the trees in the wind
the roar of a lion
the crowd cheering at the Olympics.

I will put in my box
the trunk of a tree, all knobbly and rough
the ocean so blue, the dirt in there
the memory of my dog who died last year.

I will put in my box
the sun shining on me.

My box is made of gold and metal
I will fly on my box till I come to an island
with palm trees.

Elliot Gibson (7)
Lum Head Primary School

MY MAGIC BOX

In my box I will put
The cute dog I met on holiday
The breath of a Chinese dragon
A crowd shouting at Highbury.

In my box I will put
A strange, dying star
The taste of a tub of ice cream.

I will fly in my box above the warm, sunny sky
My box is made from tigers' eyes, gems and fossils
With an icy core.

Jake Parsons-McKnight (7)
Lum Head Primary School

My Magic Box

I will put in my box
Silk soft roses
Angels' wings at the side
So I can fly across the world.

I will put in my box
Gold money
My gems in it
I will go to the rainbow.

My box is made from
Gold and silver glitter
And dogs' fluff around it.

I will keep my box
In a secret cupboard
In my room under my bed.

Leah McGahey (7)
Lum Head Primary School

MY MAGIC BOX

In my box I will put my four ugly sisters,
My chatterbox mum and dad,
My big nosed Aunty Nora,
My weak grandma and grandad.

Then I would put in my box the sound of leaves
falling to the ground,
The strong evil monster when I would see that
I will wish to die,

Then I would put in my box the sound of the snow
Falling from the sky to the ground,
Then I would put the wet fresh rain in the box.

Jinan Rabbee (7)
Lum Head Primary School

MY MAGIC BOX

I will put in my box
A gleaming star rising
The breeze of the wind
And a big chunk of bread

I will put in my box
The big shiny moon
And fresh cheese
And a goal when I score

I will put in my box
A big tree trunk
Red lava from a volcano
And a big cheetah's eye.

Ravel Ryan Moi (8)
Lum Head Primary School

POETIC VOYAGES

Today through the day of school
We did maths, English and science too.
Some days art, sometimes PE,
At 10.30 we have a break
That's the best part.

The next thing we do is maths
Numbers, plus and subtract,
We worked for an hour
It was the best subject of the day.

The end was drawing on,
Fifteen minutes till we went home.
We were finishing with something fun,
Then the bell went.

Shamimjahan Hamid (11)
Lum Head Primary School

THE MOON MEN ARE ATTACKING!

I am a space ranger
I'm protecting the Earth from danger
The moon men are attacking!
The moon men are attacking!

They are trying to send a comet to Earth
It better not hit my garden turf!
The moon men are attacking!
The moon men are attacking!

I jumped out of the ditch on the moon
The moon is sandy like a dune
The moon men are attacking!
The moon men are attacking!

I blasted the moon men with my laser
Their head popped off like a razor!
I've saved the Earth once again!
I've saved the Earth once again!

Alexander Watson (10)
Lum Head Primary School

LIFE

As I start my journey through life,
I start to cry,
I crawl around on the floor,
I try to learn more and more.

As I turn older by three years,
I learn to walk,
I learn how to talk,
What will I learn next?

As I am at school,
I can do English,
I love maths,
But I still want to learn more and more.

Becky Etel (10)
Lum Head Primary School

A JOURNEY THROUGH THE STARS

I sit and wait for my fate in the rocket
Thinking when I will go
Waiting in my head
When it will start to blow
5, 4, 3, 2, 1
Oh I hope I don't do anything wrong.

My destiny awaits at the stars
Waiting for my favourite planet Mars
Now I can see it
My mind is blowing side to side
Everything has gone wrong
The twist has started.

As I wait in the hospital
Holding my last breath
Waiting for the doctor
To do my final test
I hope the doctor will do his best.

I wish I was in Mars
Now I am in the stars
Waiting for the angel of death.

Abby Jamieson (10)
Lum Head Primary School

A Journey Through Life

First of all you learn to talk,
You can burble barble,
Then you learn to walk,
You eat the sloppy baby food
You are throwing it all over the room,
Next thing you know you're off to nursery,
Meeting other little children.
You're playing with the orange Play-doh,
You have to eat the pasta shapes,
Each day you're growing older,
And now you are in school,
Working hard on your ABCs
You are going through your years like there is no tomorrow.
Now you're in year six revising for your SATs exams!

Jessica Bergin (10)
Lum Head Primary School

TRAVELLING ACROSS THE SEA

I travel across the deep dark sea,
Wondering where I'm going to be,
Day by day I travel slow,
But where am I going to go?

The days went by so fast,
I got there at last.
I stepped out of the boat,
And I saw no one.

I walked down the road,
In a slow mode,
There is no one here,
But I feel someone is near.

Jessica Nevins (11)
Lum Head Primary School

JOURNEY TO THE HEAVENS

My whole life is a journey
But this is the longest and last of all
Going through blazing galaxies
And a cluster of planets and abundant moons
My destiny is the blissful heavens
Where life is eternal and everlasting.

Shooting stars, zooming past
Mercury orbiting the sun
Venus, the planet of love
Both lifeless and barren
Mars, known as the planet of war
And Jupiter with six wondrous moons.

Saturn, known as the ringed planet
Uranus, discovered by William Herschel
Neptune named after the god of sea
Pluto is by far the smallest of all
From here starts the golden staircase of eternity
Going up and up past galaxies.

The wondrous gates of the heavens
The fountains, mansions and gardens
All glittering merrily in the sunlight
Everything is quiet and peaceful
I'm gonna love this place
And live here forever and ever.

Thameena Chowdhury (11)
Lum Head Primary School

SHADES OF MEANING

A spirit glides through the dark night
In a house with not a speck of light.
My cover quickly covers my head
When a groaning noise comes from downstairs.
It starts from the living room
Then the hall, up the stairs and into my room.
I turn on the light and sink in my bed
And think he's not there.

Arti Parmar (10)
Lum Head Primary School

SHADES OF MEANING

A spectre creeps through the sombre night
Of your lonely cellar and hall,
And who can tell what he's looking for
Wailing with the racket of blistering wind.
'It can't be a ghost' you say to yourself
Peeping over the windowsill
But the view outside is quiet and peaceful.
The wind howls and the curtains blow
As the trees swish and the rivers flow.
The spirits fly through the ghostly mist,
Should you go outside and take the risk?
He could be in your cellar
He could be in your hall
He could be at your stairs
Or your bedroom door.

Declan Heanue (10)
Lum Head Primary School

THE HOWLING GHOST

A ghost glides through the black night
Of your deserted kitchen and hall,
And who can tell what he's seeking out,
Howling with the noise of the blowing wind.
'It can't be a ghost' you say to yourself
Peering over the windowsill -
But the garden outside is muted and placid,
No ghost now, it's morning time!

Bradley James Hough (10)
Lum Head Primary School

SHADES OF MEANING

A spirit flits through the sombre dimness,
Of your solitary attic and cellar.
And who can tell what he's seeking out,
Groaning with the racket of whooshing wind.
'It can't be a ghost' you say to yourself,
Glancing over the windowsill,
But the universe outside is muted and placid.
The wind howls through the ghostly night,
Which gives people a terrible fright.
The spooky spirits could be at the Moore,
The spooky spirits could be at your door.
They can hide under your bed,
Or over your head.
They can hide in your curtains,
Or your car instead.

Clinton Beech (10)
Lum Head Primary School

SHADES OF MEANING

A spectre creeps through the sombre dimness
Of your lonely cellar and hall,
And who can tell what he's seeking out,
Groaning with cacophony of blustering wind.
'It can't be a ghost' you say to yourself
Glancing over the windowsill
But the universe outside is muted and placid
I went back to bed holding my ted
As close as I could to my chest.

Jonathan Gregory (10)
Lum Head Primary School

IT CAN'T BE - CAN IT?

A spirit creeps through the black darkness
Of your lonely attic and hall,
And who can tell what he's seeking out for,
Howling with the noise of whooshing wind.
'It can't be a ghost' you say to yourself
Glancing over the windowsill -
But the view outside is calm and peaceful.

Now you know it's something strange,
You rush outside with the amaze,
Twelve o'clock the moonlight shows,
Mum, Dad and little sis all in bed,
With the fright you bang your head
'What was that thing?' you quietly whisper.

Kimia Etemadi (9)
Lum Head Primary School

IT CAN'T BE - CAN IT?

A spectre glides through the creepy shade,
Of your vacant attic and hall,
Who can tell what he's seeking for,
Grumbling with the effect of blasting wind.
'It can't be a ghost' you say to yourself
Peering over the windowsill -
But the universe outside is calm and motionless.
I go back to bed and close my eyes.
I dream of a lovely place like paradise,
But suddenly I hear somebody calling my name.
I sit up still and open my eyes,
And I see my mum trying to wake me up.
I ask her why she's up so early,
'It's school today my sweet old baby.'

Zahra Rabbee (10)
Lum Head Primary School

SHADES OF MEANING

A spook glides through the gloomy dimness
Of your lonely attic and cellar,
And who can tell what he's seeking out,
Shrieking with the racket of blustering wind.
'It can't be a ghost' you say to yourself
Peering over the windowsill -
But the universe outside is calm and peaceful.
I go back to bed and think is it there,
Or was it a night mare.
Then I go to bed,
Then I opened the light and heard someone
Whistling my name,
I go to bed and pull my covers over my head,
Then I write a note with a pencil but its lead is broken . . .

Chandni Arora (10)
Lum Head Primary School

SHADES OF MEANING

A spooky spirit groaning
And sighing in the pitch black night.
Swishing around the deserted hall
Searching for you.
I quickly pull the bedcovers
Over my head and wish he isn't here.
'It can't be a ghost' you say to yourself
And then they disappear.

The next night I fear
They're going to come back
No matter if it's night or day
They'll be there anyway,
They would be waiting for me
Behind an enormous old spooky tree
So I will never go out again.

Lauren Anders (9)
Lum Head Primary School

SHADES OF MEANING

A gloomy spook glides through the night.
His howling shriek brings shivers down my back.
I sink in my chair and I wish
He's gone but he's still there when I open my eyes.
So I run upstairs and into my room
And I whisper to myself
'They're not there,' and they disappeared.

The next night I fear of going outside
For they might be there
No matter if it was the night or day
They would be waiting for me in the graveyard.
So I never go out again
And that's my fear.

Francesca Wilson (10)
Lum Head Primary School

HEADLINES

When my dad was reading the paper yesterday
I read the headlines and what did it say?
Oh, it was horrible, oh gosh, oh my,
Why do people always have to die?

When my dad was reading the paper today
I read the headline and what did it say?
Oh, it was beautiful, it was lovely
It made me feel very cuddly!

When my dad reads the paper tomorrow
What will it say? What will follow?
I know I won't find out today
I have to wait another day.

Claire Hazel Greenhalgh (9)
Lum Head Primary School

IT CAN'T BE - CAN IT?

A spirit strolls through the black dimness
Of your vacant living room and hall
And who will know what he's searching for
Shrieking for the effect of blasting wind,
'It can't be a ghost' you say to yourself
Peering over the windowsill
But the space outside is noiseless and serene

You take one more look
As you see something white
You see a house or two through it
As you shiver with fright
As you're frozen with fright you can't move a muscle
Everyone's asleep, what can I do?
The ghost comes out and says
'There are worms under your bed!'

Sanna Fazal Aziz (10)
Lum Head Primary School

MY MAGIC BOX

I will put in my box
A cat in the box
You can see a curry
You can see a rose
A flag in the box
A clock in a box
You can see a paper.

Danyial Malik (7)
Lum Head Primary School

MY MAGIC BOX

I will put in my box
The touch of a wrinkled baby hand
And the good memories
of my great grandad

I will put in my box . . .
The very nice smile of all nine teachers
Especially Mrs Walls, Mrs Halls and Mrs Berryman,
They are the best
And my chuckling nannas and grandads,
The scent of 1000 flowers tickling my face.

My box is made of . . .
Wood with tiger skin
And it has a lock and key
And in case I lose the key
There is a secret ruby to open it.

Ash-leigh McDowell (8)
Lum Head Primary School

MY MAGIC BOX

I will put in my box
An angel called Zoe,
A dog's fur,
I will put in my box
Silky, soft flowers,
I will go to the rainbow,
My box is made from gold.

Natalie Mallender (7)
Lum Head Primary School

MY MAGIC BOX

I will put in my box
My Game Boy

I will put in my box
The sound of the sea

Jumping off and over the sharks
And when I have had enough

I will look up and pray to God
I am in church
And I will dive into the sea

In my box I will put my mum and dad
Jibber jabbering.

Darius Furniss (8)
Lum Head Primary School